The Invisible Premium

Why Some Companies Get Better Offers!

INTELLIGENTEXIT®
THE M&A VALUE CREATION™ PLATFORM

Discovery Exit Planning Building Value Readiness Deal Management Successful Exit

John C. Henberger, Jr.
IntelligentExit® Coach

The ideas, frameworks, methodologies, terminology, and perspectives presented in this book are the original intellectual property of the author and are shared for educational and informational purposes only. They reflect the author's professional experience and judgment developed over decades of ownership, advisory, and transaction work with privately held businesses. This material does not constitute legal, tax, accounting, investment, or other professional advice. Readers should consult their own professional advisors before making decisions based on the content of this book.

For information regarding discounts for bulk purchases or promotional applications of this book, contact rob@writeawaybooks.com.

WRITE AWAY BOOKS
Taking Authors From Idea to Manuscript to Marketplace ™

Printed in the United States of America
Published by Write Away Books
PO Box 1681, Carlsbad, CA 92018
www.writeawaybooks.com

Book design by Beth Hutchins Design, Lakeside, CA

ISBN: 978-1-969838-02-6
First Edition

MORE BOOKS IN THE WORKS BY JOHN C. HENBERGER

The ***Build a Better Business...and Sell It for More!***™ series

- The Building Value Edition (due Q4 2026)
- The Transaction Edition (due Q3 2027)
- The Regret Prevention Edition (due Q3 2028)

For Sharon.

TABLE OF CONTENTS

Opening Note:
A TALE OF TWO COMPANIES

Two companies look the same on paper, but one sells for $10 million and the other for $7 million. What do you think the buyer saw that the financials did not show?

This scenario unfolds more times than most owners would expect.

Two companies enter the market from the same industry. Revenue is similar, and margins are comparable. The financials are clean, and from the owners' perspective both companies feel successful. Both owners believe they've done the hard work.

Only one business sells for **$10 million**, while the other closes at **$7 million**.

There are no major issues behind the gap. Performance holds. Customers stay. Due diligence confirms the numbers. Yet buyers lean in on one business…and hesitate on the other.

That hesitation didn't start at the negotiating table. Rather, it started much earlier - in how the buyer *experienced* the business.

Because buyers don't just analyze results; they imagine ownership. They ask themselves - often quietly - the following questions:

- *Will this business hold together without the owner?*
- *Will customers stay?*

- *Will the earnings repeat themselves?*
- *Will I spend my time managing growth or managing risk?*

These types of questions shape value in the buyer's mind long before price is discussed. Because this is where goodwill actually lives.

Not goodwill as an accounting entry recorded at the end of a transaction, but goodwill as an economic expression of confidence that the business is durable, transferable, predictable, and easy to own.

The $10 million business answers those questions without being asked, while the $7 million business leaves room for doubt.

From the seller's side of the table, the difference can feel frustrating…or even unfair. From the buyer's side, it feels prudent.

This gap is what I call the **Invisible Premium**.

It's the value buyers assign to what doesn't show up on the financials but strongly influences how safe the future feels. It explains why businesses with similar performance produce very different outcomes for their owners.

This book is meant to spark better conversations between owners and advisors. These are discussions about how value is actually formed in a buyer's mind, and what can be done *years in advance* to influence that outcome.

They recognize that something is only worth as much as someone is willing to pay for it.

Therefore, the most important question isn't *"What is my business worth today?"* It's *"What will a buyer believe about it when I'm no longer in the room?"*

The Context of this Collection

This collection is written for entrepreneurs who are intentionally building, protecting, and preparing to transfer the value of their business at some point.

Owners experience trade secrets, brand strength, and recurring revenue as part of running the business, while buyers experience these same elements differently. To a buyer, they are signs that earnings will persist, advantages will endure, and that the business can transition without undue risk.

The sections that follow explain why these signs matter and why they quietly compound. Individually, they may seem familiar. Collectively, they will shape confidence in the future and help explain why some businesses command better offers than others.

This collection is intentionally nonprescriptive. It is not a how-to manual or a set of technical solutions. Instead, it provides a lens for understanding where value is created and how buyer perceptions influence pricing, deal terms, and certainty of closing.

Professional advisors play a critical role in turning this understanding into action. This collection supports clearer conversations between owners and advisors, stronger alignment across disciplines, and more intentional value creation well before a transaction is considered.

The content is presented as selected readings, and sections may be reviewed independently or in sequence. After all, the intent here is not to replace professional advice, but to improve how a potential seller's decisions are framed and discussed.

PART I
INTELLECTUAL PROPERTY

What You Will Learn About Trade Secrets, Brand Equity, and Recurring Revenue

This collection helps owners understand why some businesses get better offers, even when financial performance appears similar on paper to other companies. As you move through the sections that follow, you will learn:

- **How buyers interpret non-financial signs** such as trade secrets, brand strength, and operational continuity, and why those signs often matter as much as - or perhaps even more than - reported earnings
- **Why confidence compounds** in a buyer's mind, and how (when taken together) familiar elements influence pricing, deal structure, and the certainties of closing the deal
- **How perceived risk shapes offers**, including where uncertainty quietly erodes value long before a transaction begins
- **Why goodwill is not an accounting afterthought**, but a forward-looking judgment buyers make about the durability and transferability of a business
- **How buyer perceptions differ from owner experience**, and why closing that gap is central to commanding better offers
- **Where intentional decisions made years in advance** can materially improve outcomes from selling a business, even without changing headline financial results

It's important for the reader to recognize at the outset that this collection is intentionally not a how-to manual. It does not offer technical solutions or implementation instructions. Instead, it provides a practical lens for understanding how value is created, interpreted, and rewarded from a buyer's point of view.

Professional advisors play a critical role in turning these insights into action. The intent here is to support clearer owner–advisor conversations, stronger alignment across disciplines, and more intentional value creation well before a transaction is contemplated.

Perspective Note:

Throughout this collection, value is described from a buyer's point of view. This is not to favor the buyer, but to clarify how buyer perceptions ultimately shape owner outcomes and the offers they may receive.

~ CHAPTER 1 ~

TRADE SECRETS

In the last chapter of my upcoming book - The Building Value Edition of the ***Build a Better Business...and Sell It for More!***™ series - we discuss the importance of establishing and identifying key value drivers; particularly IP assets like trade secrets and brand equity.

As I wrote it I thought about my old company, and with what I know now I'd like to share some thoughts about how we could have probably done better. My expectation is you'll benefit and profit from our experience.

Here are some general examples of trade secrets from my own businesses and business life. Because we made significant investments to automate our systems, and I'm guessing your goal - like mine - has been to give you a competitive edge and grow your sales and your bottom line.

Henberger Traffic Center
Traffic Safety and Control Products

Identify and Document!

Early in 1990, my company spent about a million dollars ($2.5 million in 2026) on NT servers, new desktop computers, laptops, application software, training, travel, and expert advisors. It was a System 36-based accounting system.

In the late nineties we purchased a new Windows NT 3.1-based distribution/light manufacturing ERP system. We wanted to load all our product, process, and customer/vendor-based information onto this ERP system, but it wasn't easy. Our non-accounting information was widely distributed on internal sales laptops, vendor database files, manual systems, and other remote locations.

We figured automating our products, processes, and customer data not only would make us more efficient, but we determined it would give us a competitive edge...and we wanted to grow.

However, we missed the opportunity to show increased business value!

In retrospect, we should have designated more of our processes, proprietary information, configurations, and strategies as trade secrets. The reason I mention our ERP system is that it was integral to what we could have designated as trade secrets.

Below you will find a categorization of potential trade secrets we could have identified and developed.

- **Customer Lists and Information** - There are a lot of reasons my company should have designated items in this category as trade secrets. Some salespeople think they own the customer data, and I understand that thinking. After all, they worked hard to book the business.

But customer acquisition and relationships are a TEAM effort. Marketing gets the leads, outside sales interacts with the customers, inside sales takes and coordinates the orders, logistics pulls and gets the orders delivered, and accounting keeps the money flowing. Each sale impacts everyone, and this information can't be allowed to go to a competitor if an employee walks out the door.

If a company doesn't protect this information, they risk letting down the rest of the team. Meaning the information in this category should be designated and treated as trade secrets, making the company more valuable to an investor. You're also protecting your assets.

Thus the company's higher value would be based on how you protect vital data, let alone protecting your company and its stakeholders.

- **Business Strategies, Forecasts, and Marketing Plans** - Our unique sales team forecasting of sales and profits by vendor, customer, product, and projects was not only proprietary, but incredibly strategic to our success. Not only did it give us management insights, but we also provided select sales information to our principals. It allowed our customers, our principals, and our company to negotiate favorable prices to help build our customers' success. Our customers viewed us more as partners than merely as vendors. And with this proprietary knowledge of their operations, we had an obligation to protect their information.

For many of the same reasons as applied to customer lists, these plans and strategies should have been selectively designated and protected as trade secrets. They gave us a competitive edge by forging a stronger partnership with our customers, principals, and other stakeholders, which in turn built increased trust in our brand.

- **Internal Processes, including manufacturing and operations** - In our industry, we were universally considered to be both innovators and pioneers. One of our companies was known for its PC-based automation products and value-add systems. Many of our assembly and manufacturing processes were unique, and we developed significant efficiencies.

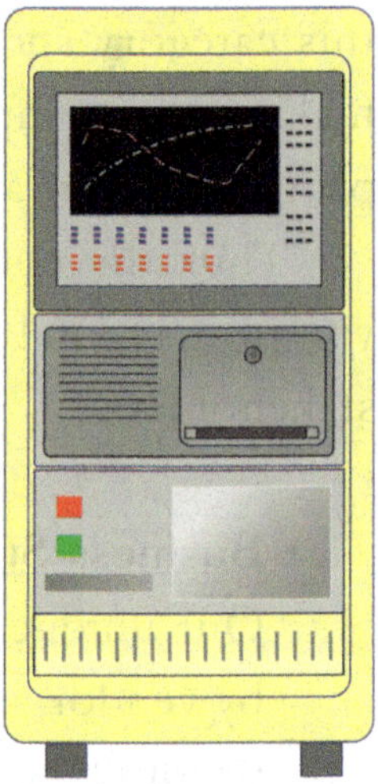

We were, in fact, the largest industrial computer distributor in southern California and, most likely, the western region. Documenting value-add products, processes, and strategies would have added value from an investor's point of view. These strategies would have shown potential investors a strong management team.

Meaning if you can designate select products and processes as trade secrets, it'll add additional value to the company and protect the company's strategies as proprietary intellectual property.

- **Software and Algorithms** - We built what we called "golden disks" for customer IBM Industrial Computer configurations - what today would be called a process algorithm. This was helpful with orders containing large quantities and identical configurations, while assuring delivery of error-free quality products. This gave us a unique competitive advantage, and we always insisted on tight customer coordination. Had we been for sale and had designated these proprietary processes as trade secrets, it would have been highly valued by prospective investors. It would have lent an aura of respect to our processes and our management team, leading to a higher valuation and offer. You can count on your M&A transaction advisor to tell this part of your company story…but YOU need to tell them about it first.

- **Principal and Customer Agreements** - We securely kept all our contracts with principals, vendors and customers - electronically and hard copies - on file. All the information was proprietary and should have been designated as Trade Secrets to protect these assets. **You don't want them to ever walk out the door!**

- **Product Designs and Prototypes** - We built custom computer prototypes and value-add products. This included rack-mounting an industrial PC on a custom, rolling, rack-mount cabinet for automotive brake measuring applications for auto mechanics' retail shops. This assembly was also used in other applications where mobility on the factory floor was a benefit, such as paperless manufacturing.

Of course this was before iPhones, iPads, and other mobile devices.

We also didn't legally protect these assemblies. Some components were patented by others and could have been integrated into our own proprietary assemblies.

Now I realize we could have designated these industrial computer assemblies as trade secrets - especially combined with software and measurement instruments - only it never even occurred to us. Our focus was more on building revenue, rather than company value. In hindsight, I realize that building value should have been a **paramount** consideration, and on par with revenue.

- **Paint and Chemicals** - At Henberger Traffic Center, we sold some paint industry-related products for customer applications. Of particular note were the traffic paint and pump-based applicators; part of a line of paint stripers used in parking lots or street marking that we developed and that arguably could have been patentable. We decided that because of the volume and the competitive environment, it made financial sense to offer these additional products to help us sell more traffic paint.

- **<u>Training Methods and Operational Procedures</u>** - We had fee-based internal classroom training classes for the software and high-tech hardware products we distributed. We also provided application training for the software driver products that we developed. Our software drivers were apps we didn't want to patent, as they would show our competition some of our more unique approaches and algorithms. Combined - and again, in hindsight - I believe some of our training methods, despite reliance on manufacturer basic training materials, were unique. This made them perfect candidates for designating them as trade secrets.

- **<u>Innovations protected as trade secrets</u>** - We wrote specific drivers for third-party customer equipment interfacing with computers, input/output devices, and automation software that we sold, created, and distributed. Some of them were quite innovative, and I realize now that the drivers and products were something we could have designated as trade secrets, but didn't because of volume constraints and our focus on sales revenue.

> Besides, at the time we didn't even think about it because of the relatively low system volumes. Our goal was to sell more of our products: IBM Industrial PCs, automation software, instrumentation, and PC-related products…and it did.

The important point here is that trade secrets can be a valuable asset for any company. Considerations when designating functions or products as trade secrets should be your assessment of the competitive environment and determining if the cost of development, marketing , and the resources required to maintain them as trade secrets adds to the company's value. Certainly (and from a legal costs perspective), documenting trade secrets can be less costly than a patent. But the question should always be whether it will give you enough of a competitive edge while also protecting your inventions.

So ask yourself whether your trade secrets have enough value to you that keeping them secret helps you maintain a competitive edge? Will they protect your company? Because protecting your company protects company value.

Also, don't forget the overall mission is to create business value; the value that makes your business more investor-worthy. It is something that will deliver stability and future growth for your stakeholders.

~ CHAPTER 2 ~

BRAND EQUITY

Let's talk about Brand Equity and how it affected our businesses. But first, some key points about brand awareness, brand trust, and brand equity.

Brand Awareness - Brand awareness reflects visibility and recognition in the market, as it shows that a company is known, remembered, and considered. However awareness alone is structurally weak, because without trust, awareness attracts attention but does not reduce investor risk. In an IntelligentExit®, awareness is necessary but insufficient; it is the surface layer, not the value layer.

In other words, brand awareness gets you noticed.

Brand Trust - Brand trust reflects confidence earned through consistent delivery, reliability, and integrity. It reduces perceived execution, customer, and revenue risk. However, trust that lacks awareness is under-leveraged. That is, it exists but too few stakeholders know it is there. In an IntelligentExit®, trust stabilizes earnings and customer relationships, but it must be visible to fully translate into value.

Put another way, brand trust makes you credible.

Brand Equity - Brand equity is the economic expression of awareness and trust combined. It represents the portion of enterprise value because of reputation, loyalty, pricing power, and durability of relationships. In an IntelligentExit®, brand equity is not a branding concept; it is monetized confidence. Buyers pay for it because it lowers risk, supports multiple expansion, and increases certainty of future cash flows.

In short, brand equity makes your business valuable.

Examples of Brand Awareness, Brand Trust, and Brand Equity

Here are a few examples of brand awareness, brand trust, and brand equity in action. Of course, brand awareness can lead to brand trust, and when combined and properly planned, they may even rise to brand equity.

Customer Loyalty to a Brand. I'm going to use my Dad as an example. My Dad was a passionate fan of the San Diego Chargers, and San Diegans like him are proud of our city. In 1961 - to the excitement of our community and after just one year in Los Angeles - the AFL Chargers team moved to San Diego! The excellent Super Chargers, no less. It was a real boost to the San Diego citizenry, as we were constantly smarting from LA's "put-downs" of San Diego as a backwater and little more than an LA suburb. Naturally, we were ecstatic that the Chargers preferred San Diego as their home, as we would now have our own AFL big-time football team!

Brand Trust Damaged. In the early sixties, San Diegans went crazy for the Super Chargers and their coach Sid Gillman as they won five AFL West Championships, including one Conference Championship. My Dad bought two season tickets at Balboa Stadium for the first day they played in San Diego. As they moved to the Murph[1] (later Qualcomm Stadium), he bought four - then six - tickets, and held them until the day he died. He even bet on them to win during the many years they were terrible. **Talk about loyalty!**

I am just glad he didn't have to see that horrible day in 2017 when the Spanos family sold the City of San Diego down the river and moved the team back to Los Angeles. No doubt Dean Spanos hates surfing and golf, as these are the sports many San Diegans now prefer to enjoy every Sunday, rather than watching the LA (ugh!) Chargers play football.

Awareness of a Brand and Reputation. The name LA Chargers still stings, although some of us still like the players and sneak a peek on the television now and then. However, the owner's reputation is garbage to true San Diegans, and many of us still avoid supporting them. Them having a great coach in Jim Harbaugh will help, as he is well known to San Diegans as he used to coach the University of San Diego's Torero football team's success before he moved to Stanford, the Niners, and Michigan. Despite this potentially mitigating factor, though, because for true San Diegans the Chargers brand is forever damaged.

Customer Perception of Quality. Perception of quality is how a customer views, judges, and enjoys the experience of doing business with a company or using their branded products. For instance, LVMH (Moët Hennessy Louis Vuitton) is instantly recognized as one of the great worldwide luxury brands of champagne, cognac, fashion, and more. Consumers who can afford their products pay extra for the quality and prestige they represent.

Brand Halo Effect. LVMH uses the halo effect of offering highly desirable luxury products to extend a sense of prestige over other company brands and products. This halo effect drives sales across the product spectrum for LVMH, and even casts a halo over any new category and product introductions they bring out.

LVMH isn't the only one to use this idea to their advantage. For example, in the seventies and eighties, there was a saying in the business community that "No one ever got fired for specifying or buying IBM."

Brand Trust. Vehicles, clothing, marketing materials, signage, all with a standardized image and overall messaging umbrella. Take Stanley Steemer, for example, which is best known as a home carpet cleaning service and uses its brand identification as a badge of safety and reliability. It is a sign that the consumer is getting the genuine experience, and the company touts that they always provide their service in a well-marked yellow van, with their people wearing red shirts and white trousers. This strategy not only identifies the company, but encourages loyalty and a sense of safety. Stanley Steemer[2] has grown to over 280 franchise locations. This consistency of messaging reinforcing the brand helps explain why my wife Sharon always uses Stanley Steemer, because they're constantly reinforcing the value that they bring to their customers.

Long-Term Customer and Principal[3] Relationships. Investors highly value long-term relationships, whether they're with customers, vendors, or principals (vendor mutual product marketing partnerships). However, a note of caution is in order: don't let your customers or principal relationships get concentrated and become too big a part of your overall business. Because as sure as my name is John Henberger, if that relationship ends abruptly, your company could find itself in an unpleasant position, or even face potential for brand equity catastrophe.

Furthermore, to ensure you're maintaining good customer relations and providing the services and products that people want, be sure to regularly survey and document customer loyalty and opinions. After all, you can never know enough about those to whom you are selling.

So how do your company's trade secrets and brand equity positively affect business value when you are considering an exit?

During the Building Value phase of the IntelligentExit®, brand equity strengthens and differentiates your company. While in the Readiness phase, brand equity should be shown by documenting it during readiness and for due diligence. And during Deal Management, brand equity should be communicated to prospective buyers as reduced buyer risk and how the company's brand equity has a positive upside.

But here's the bottom line: Well-developed trade secret and brand equity strategies enhance the image of your company's quality, reliability, and value. It shows the management team's effectiveness and transferability, both of which are highly valued by investors.

Your company will be recognized for these positive attributes, and this will create and expand trust in your brand(s). It can both significantly differentiate your company AND provide a competitive edge over your competition.

All these attributes are prized by prospective investors looking to buy your business. They value a company with an outstanding reputation, but - maybe more importantly - they desire a company that will continue to grow business value well after the sale is completed.

Let's also look at the example of why recurring revenue using your trade secrets and brand equity strategies can drive business value.

But first, a quick question: how soon should you start this process? Quite simply, that is up to you. If you are within ten years of selling your business, or you plan to transfer it to insiders, then I would argue you should already be working on your strategy.

SO LET'S GET TO WORK!

[1] Author's note: San Diego Jack Murphy Stadium - nicknamed "The Murph" - was named after a longtime San Diego Union sports writer and masterful booster of all things related to San Diego. Jack was prominent in helping to bring both the Chargers and the Padres to San Diego.

[2] Stanley Steemer website, https://www.stanleysteemer.com

[3] Author's note: as a refresher, principals are supplier/partners when you distribute a product and resell it. An example for our family business was IBM Industrial Computers; we called them a Principal because we had shared interest in selling - not just using - their products.

~ CHAPTER 3 ~

DRIVING BUSINESS VALUE

Brand equity refers to the perceived value associated with the company brand name, reputation, and how the market views the company, providing an aura surrounding your company. Brand Equity is not an IP asset, per se, though it IS an intangible asset that potentially contains two important IP asset classes: Copyrights and Trademarks. Arguably, you might also include Trade Secrets in there.

A better valuation is achieved because strong brand equity drives customer loyalty, allowing premium pricing and higher profits. Tending to brand equity sustains and promotes company stability. Copyrights and trademarks are legal rights, and play an important part in brand equity. They can tangibly affect the value of brand equity, since brand equity value results from a long-term investment in marketing, customer care, and your IP strategies.

Why does brand equity drive business value?

Well-established brand equity as an asset can drive the ability to charge premium prices, with increased revenue and profit margins. It does this through company marketing and promotion, protecting trademarks, copyrights, and trade secrets. All components of brand equity - promoting stories of positive customer experiences, excellent systems, and developing customer principal partnering programs - can encourage repeat business and a long-term promise of customer retention.

How does brand equity affect an exit strategy?

A high-performing company with significant brand equity is highly valued by investors. It is because the company will be viewed as a stable platform for future growth well after the acquisition and the owner has exited.

Well-documented, time-tested, positive brand equity leads to higher valuations based on higher multiples and increased EBITDA.

It will deliver a higher valuation with prospects for a better company future.

~ CHAPTER 4 ~

A PERSONAL CASE STUDY

If you are considering a sale or transfer of your business, start your planning early - well before you put it on the market. Evaluate your internal processes, manual systems, value-add service methods, and proprietary business techniques. Evaluate them with an IP valuation expert, a branding specialist, and your IP attorney to see how documenting your trade secrets and brand equity will work for you.

For example, one of our family-owned companies was an IBM Industrial Computer distributor. Our customers often ordered these industrialized PCs configured to their requirements, with configurations that included operating systems, proprietary software, and third-party PC-based hardware accessories. We often sold dozens, if not hundreds, of these systems for customer projects, and our customers wanted us to deliver the completed, configured systems directly to their manufacturing line, bypassing receiving. We became part of their internal manufacturing process as a business partner, bypassing the receiving department and eliminating a costly, potentially duplicative step in their process.

To do this, and following their manufacturing process, we would document and follow our customer-certified internal processes, saving our customers time and money. We followed our own customer-approved ISO 9001 quality process and our documented internal procedures, burn-ins, and testing methods, and our goal was the same as our customer's - delivering a cost-efficient, error-free solution. We spent a lot of time designing and documenting our systems to accommodate these goals. Our process included our company's internal IT systems, using designated areas in our building, and limited access to those assembly areas. The design of these systems was our own R&D process.

We could have documented some of these processes as trade secrets.

Our processes were unknown to our competitors, giving us a competitive edge because of special processes and pricing. At the time we didn't even think of it as a trade secret, but just did it because it drove revenue and repeat business.

If we were to sell our company, well-documented and proprietary processes would have added to the business value, and even more so if they were designated as a trade secret. It drove repeat sales and better profits, not only for us but for our customers. These were attributes that would have been valued by investors.

Today I believe you should always have your business in a high state of readiness for a potential sale. Developing and documenting your trade secrets should start now.

After all, you never know when you might get an offer.

Besides, if you are not transaction-ready every day, you start negotiations at an immediate disadvantage. You are guaranteed to not get the best offer, nor will you get an outrageously great price. Because the fact is that without trade secret or brand equity documentation, an investor may not consider these items to be of value. They may negotiate a lower price during due diligence if you don't tell them about them and prove it through written documentation.

Meaning you'll easily find that you are not in full control of the process.

Today, I would advise my younger self to take the extra steps to identify, develop, and document our trade secrets and other intellectual property. It takes time...so the sooner you start, the better.

Finally, if you are thinking of selling your business at some point, I recommend you take steps now to ready your business.[1] Inform your advisory team about your exit timetable, and start WELL before you put the business on the market. Don't forget to talk to an M&A transaction advisor early on so you understand their process and learn how they can help you target the right buyer types. Tell them about the entire scope of these important assets so that together you can tell the entire company story and establish a higher company value.

The obvious point: to show that you have built a better business!

In the following chapters I'll introduce some additional features that show trade secrets and brand equity assets. The experiences are from my family's businesses, as well as from decades of extensive general business experience.

[1] Author's note, see the chapter "How to Develop, then Start an M&A Value Creation™ Strategy for Your Business." This chapter can be found in the new book *THE BUILDING VALUE EDITION* of the Series *Build a Better Business...and Sell It for More!*

~ CHAPTER 5 ~

RECURRING REVENUE

Recurring revenue is one of the most powerful expressions of intellectual property. It creates predictability, stability, and confidence; qualities that investors value deeply and owners benefit from long before any transaction occurs. When recurring or re-occurring revenue is well designed, it becomes a compounding engine that supports both operational resilience and enterprise value. Recurring and re-occurring revenue is typically built through one or more of the following models:

- Subscriptions where customers pay regularly and revenue compounds
- Contract-based revenue tied to long-term agreements, such as usage-based revenue models like cloud services
- Licensing and royalty income derived from intellectual property
- Maintenance and service plans that extend customer relationships beyond the initial sale

- Consumables or replenishment products that customers purchase repeatedly as part of their normal operations

The most valued recurring revenue models are those that continue year after year. Revenue compounds as new customers are added and customer churn is minimized. Investors favor businesses with these kinds of predictable, growing cash flows and accelerating recurring revenue streams.

Plus when customer acquisition costs are controlled, this type of revenue also drives stronger EBITDA, and strong EBITDA supported by predictable revenue often commands higher valuation multiples.

In short, greater EBITDA with a higher multiple is a powerful indicator of successful value creation.

A case from our M&A transaction advisory practice illustrates this point clearly. We worked with an audio-visual (AV)/installation company that - prior to going to market - explored creating a recurring revenue stream. AV systems monitoring combines software with installed hardware that allows systems to be monitored remotely. While there was limited time to show long-term financial results, the goal was to enhance stability and reinforce buyer confidence in the management team.

To their credit, our client embraced the concept. They conducted research; brought the management team together; developed marketing and sales strategies; formed partnerships for monitoring equipment and software; implemented the plan; and validated the concept with customers...all within a few months.

It was very exciting to watch.

The company replaced a traditional one-year maintenance agreement with a recurring revenue, system monitoring model.

Customers received real-time oversight of installed systems, proactive alerts, preventative actions, and monthly reports from our client. Quarterly face-to-face review meetings reinforced the value of uptime and positioned the service as mission-critical.

A dedicated team and profit center were built around the program, and customer confidence grew over time. Downtime decreased, and renewal rates improved.

Thus while the impact of the recurring revenue model on company value was limited because of the relatively short time the program had been in existence, the strategic impact was not. The management team showed foresight, planning capability, and execution discipline…and it mattered. **A LOT!**

Recurring revenue models typically require three to five years to be fully validated. Investors want proof of concept, rather than just good ideas. Here, the effort reinforced management credibility and reduced perceived risk. During due diligence, the originally offered price held firm. And despite moments where both parties stepped away from negotiations, the quality of the business and its preparation ultimately cemented the transaction. The buyer - a large private equity platform company - recognized the durability of the enterprise.

In the end, our client was satisfied with the outcome.

Here's the bottom line: predictable revenue, disciplined execution, and documented systems are powerful drivers of enterprise value. However, intellectual property may not create lasting value if it's tied to one person, rather than to the company as a whole.

~ CHAPTER 6 ~

THE ODDITIES OF YOUR PERSONAL BRAND

When I refer to oddities, I am talking about something I see far too often. A business owner's Personal Brand Value (PBV) becomes so tightly wrapped around the axle of the company that the two are almost indistinguishable from each other. What should move freely binds. This creates a significant concern when an owner thinks seriously about selling or transferring the business. The challenge and the opportunity is turning personal brand into transferable brand value for the company.

My point? PBV can become a negative value driver if it's not made transferable, and any business owner ignores this concept at their own risk.

This perspective comes from having lived on both sides of the table. You see, I spent years as a middle-market business owner and later founded an investment banking firm, working as an M&A transaction advisor and Exit Planning consultant. Over time I have worked with sophisticated investors and surrounded myself with experts at the top of their respective fields. That experience shapes how I view personal brand value; not emotionally, but economically.

Of course, personal brand value is difficult to define, measure, and transfer. And when it cannot be easily transferred, it typically becomes more of a value detractor rather than a value creator. If PBV cannot be clearly explained, documented, or institutionalized, buyers will discount the business or walk away altogether.

One common form of personal brand value is star power. A familiar example is George Clooney and Casamigos Tequila. Casamigos was founded by Clooney, Rande Gerber, and Mike Meldman - three successful entrepreneurs who clearly did not need the money.

From the outside, the brand appeared to have begun as a passion project fueled by friendship and a relentless pursuit of quality. The three owners reportedly worked long into the night conducting "research" (wink! wink!) to achieve exactly what they were looking for. They were also so firmly committed to the company's success that, even after the sale, the founders remained closely involved.

This discussion is not about Casamigos, though. It is about the importance of converting personal brand value to transferable brand value.

Clooney's notoriety enhanced brand awareness, which is classic personal brand value. Yet what mattered to the buyer was not celebrity, but whether the brand could endure independently. Keeping the founders post-sale made sense, but the value was in the brand's ability to persist long after their involvement ended.

Many business owners have star power in their own markets, with customers doing business with the company because of the owner. That can be enormously valuable...until it isn't. When the owner leaves and the star power leaves with them, the company's value prospects often dim or evaporate.

Consider the CEO who makes all the key decisions and serves as the primary salesperson. At some point this concentration of authority becomes a negative value driver. Decision-making must broaden. Sales must extend beyond a one-person show. Otherwise, dependency becomes a discount.

Personal brand value also shows up in intelligence and perseverance. Most successful owners are intelligent risk-takers but what differentiates them is their persistence. Over time, however, habits formed during early survival stages must evolve, with strategic planning, team development, and shared decision-making becoming essential.

We often hear that it is better to be lucky than good. In my experience, sustained success comes from competence colliding with opportunity and being smart enough to capitalize on it.

Converting personal brand value into transferable brand value should be an intentional strategy during the Build Value and Transaction Readiness phases. Clooney's star power created awareness, but systems, trust, and execution created equity. That distinction matters.

Because personal brand value can help build a business, but only transferable brand value allows it to endure. Recognizing this kind of friction often changes how owners think about what they have built and what must come next.

~ CHAPTER 7 ~

THOUGHTS ABOUT BRAND TRUST AND ITS TRANSFERABILITY

Recognizing the difference between personal brand value and transferable brand value often causes business owners to pause. It changes how they think about what they have built and what it means for the future. This chapter is not about tactics or checklists, but more about reflection, perspective, and the journey that allows value to stand on its own.

When your personal brand is deeply stamped into the brand of your company, it is a challenge to migrate your personal brand into value that can stand on its own. The process can prove difficult, but it is essential for long-term sustainability and scalability, let alone business value.

Over time, the goal is for what begins as personal brand value to become company-owned brand value - capable of standing and growing on its own. It thus becomes critically important to ensure your personal brand becomes the company's brand so the company brand value can continue to thrive on its own after you're no longer in the picture.

Because the reality is that the company's long-term viability and value depend on making this journey. Doing it correctly will have an impact not only on your personal wealth, but also the future of your employees, customers, and other stakeholders.

Speaking of journeys, I love fly-fishing in the Sierras… especially along the Middle Fork of the San Joaquin. The stretch I like extends downstream from Agnew Meadows, past the Devil's Postpile, to a mile or three below Rainbow Falls. A good portion of these waters is designated Wild Trout Waters. You may have your own favorite spots for fishing. For me, the beauty, serenity, flora and fauna, and especially the wild trout make these my favorite waters, particularly from mid-June to mid-October.

Fly-fishing is challenging. After all, you have to outsmart a trout with a brain smaller than a BB. However, you are in their house. You have to pay attention to the hatch, the time of day, and how the river flows through the boulders. You also need to watch out for those nasty willow trees that snag your fly, interrupt your serenity, and sometimes prevent your success in landing a trout.

Fly-fishing is not only challenging because of the wariness of the trout, but I also make it challenging for myself. Like Rush Limbaugh, I metaphorically fish with one hand tied behind my back. I crimp the barbs on all my flies, wade into alternately hastening and placid waters, and navigate slippery rocks. I take my time along the trail or wading down the middle of the river, watching for pine martens, black bears, deer, raptors, and other critters. The flowers lining the banks and the Fisherman's Trail from early July through late August are spectacular. During the golden hour, the hatch rises in the late afternoon, and the white flecks of mayflies glow against the golden tones of the sky.

I enjoy turning over rocks while maintaining my balance in rushing water to see what the trout are feeding on. A fisherman needs to figure out what the trout are munching on and dig into the kit for just the right kind of fly - dry or wet - because what the trout are eating really matters.

Part of my fly-fishing day usually includes walking the John Muir Trail - particularly the Devil's Postpile segment. The John Muir Trail is perhaps the most famous trail in the United States, and intersects with the Pacific Crest Trail. Backpackers move up and down the two trails navigating their own journeys, sharing it with fly-fishing interlopers and happily chatting about critter sightings and trout holes just around the bend. New friendships form easily, and when we're out there we'll oftentimes invite our new friends to stop by our camp to share an adult beverage or some s'mores around a roaring fire at Pumice Flat Campground. On clear nights the sky is breathtaking, accompanied by the sound of the San Joaquin winding through granite boulders and willow trees.

To enjoy fly-fishing and do it right takes preparation and planning. It starts with what to pack in your kit or camper and continues with planning each day and strategizing your approach. As I mentioned earlier, "success is the intersection of competence colliding with luck™," though it also requires being smart enough to capitalize on that moment.

Oh, in case you wondered, I always release the wild trout I catch so they can outwit someone else another day, or perhaps return the following year as a bigger, wiser nemesis willing to challenge me. And when that moment comes, I release the trout—not because it wasn't earned, but because that's the point.

The journey to transfer your personal brand into a brand that can stand on its own is much the same. Whether your brand was a burly seven-pound brown trout or your first Sierra Slam, you can look back with pride at what you have accomplished. But if you hold on too tightly, the value remains dependent on you, and becomes counter-productive. So as you plan your exit, now is the time to release your brand and your company back into the wild waters of the marketplace. When you release it - by documenting what you know, sharing decisions, and building capability in others - the value will have a chance to continue, grow, and be owned by the business itself.

The same patience, preparation, and respect for process that make fly-fishing successful are required when transforming personal brand value into transferable brand value and intellectual property that can stand on its own.

I loved sharing my passion for fly-fishing with my son Jason while he was growing up, and today he is a far better angler than I am. In much the same way, there is satisfaction in watching others grow into leadership and stewardship roles within a business. Taking pride in what you've built does not require holding on tightly. More often, it requires letting go.

As you reflect on this section on intellectual property, consider not only what you have built, but whether it has been designed to endure. These reflections can help prepare you for an understanding of the buyer's perspective in this section.

The next chapter summarizes the key lessons from the intellectual property section and highlights the takeaways that will shape how you think about value, transferability, and long-term success.

~ CHAPTER 8 ~

INTELLECTUAL PROPERTY

This section shows that intellectual property is not an abstract legal category, but rather a primary driver of invisible value. Buyers pay attention to intellectual property because it answers a fundamental question: *what makes this business defensible, repeatable, and worth owning after the founder exits?*

You've seen that trade secrets and proprietary know-how often matter more than formal registrations, provided they are protected, documented, and embedded in the organization. You've also seen how brand equity converts trust into economic value by stabilizing customer behavior, reducing friction, and supporting long-term performance. When brand equity is institutional rather than personal, it strengthens goodwill. When it lives only in the founder, it introduces risk.

Recurring revenue models further show how intellectual property can be transformed into predictable cash flow. By turning systems, relationships, and know-how into repeatable revenue streams, businesses make future earnings feel safer and more durable.

The discussion of personal brand value highlights an important tension. While an owner's reputation can speed up growth, it can also limit transferability if it is not intentionally separated from the business itself.

The overarching lesson from all this is that intellectual property must be designed for continuity, rather than just for success. In an IntelligentExit®, IP becomes a strategic asset when it survives ownership change, supports predictable revenue, and reinforces confidence in the business' future. When treated casually, informally, or personally, it becomes a value reducer rather than a value multiplier.

This section closes with a simple but powerful conclusion: intellectual property creates its greatest value when it can stand on its own.

Key Takeaways

- Intellectual property is a core pillar of M&A Value Creation™, not an accessory.
- Trade secrets are hidden assets: when documented and protected, they increase buyer confidence.
- Brand equity converts customer trust into tangible economic value.
- Recurring revenue is strongest when powered by IP-based systems and durable brand loyalty.
- Transferring personal brand value to the company enhances value and exit readiness.
- Creative programs, partnerships, and systems can extend and reinforce your brand beyond the founder.
- Protect, document, and show intellectual property. Because buyers invest in certainty, not assumptions.

PART II
INVESTORS' PERSPECTIVE

How an Investor's
Point of View
Creates Value.

With a clear understanding of how intellectual property creates value, the next step is to see how that value is judged. This section helps owners understand how investors think when evaluating why some businesses command better offers, even when financial performance appears similar on paper, and will help you learn:

- How buyers interpret non-financial signs such as trade secrets, brand strength, recurring revenue, and operational continuity, and why these signs often matter as much as reported earnings
- Why confidence compounds in a buyer's mind, and how familiar, reinforcing elements taken together influence pricing, deal structure, and certainty of closing the deal.
- How perceived risk shapes offers, including where uncertainty quietly erodes value long before a transaction begins
- Why goodwill is not an accounting afterthought, but a forward-looking judgment buyers make about the durability and transferability of a business
- How buyer perceptions differ from owner experience, and why closing that gap is central to commanding better offers
- Where intentional decisions made years in advance can materially improve outcomes, even without changing headline financial results

This section is intentionally not a checklist, nor does it provide technical solutions or implementation instructions. Instead, it offers a practical lens for understanding how investors interpret value, confidence, and risk when forming offers.

Professional advisors play a critical role in translating these insights into action. This perspective is intended to support clearer owner/advisor conversations; stronger alignment across disciplines; and more intentional value creation well before a transaction is contemplated.

Perspective Note:

Throughout this book, value is described from a buyer's point of view. This is not to favor the buyer, but to clarify how buyer perceptions ultimately shape owner outcomes, deal terms, and offers.

~ CHAPTER 9 ~

THE INVESTOR'S POINT OF VIEW

Based on my experience, every successful exit requires seeing your business through the eyes of an investor. Understanding how investors think, what they value, what they fear, and how they assess opportunity are all central to building a business that commands better offers and results in cleaner deals.

The reality is that financial performance matters, but it is rarely the sole determinant of a deal's outcome. What ultimately shapes valuation, deal structure, and certainty of closing is how investors interpret what they see and what they believe will endure after the founder steps away.

This section explores the investor's point of view and why it matters to your IntelligentExit® and your M&A Value Creation™ strategies. The goal is not to teach you how to negotiate or to replace professional advisors, but instead to help you connect your preparation, performance, and positioning. Because these are to the criteria investors actually use when assigning value and evaluating risk in any opportunity, and they're sure to have a huge potential impact on your personal fortunes moving forward.

Here's the thing: investors must constantly balance risk and return as they look for new directions worth exploring opportunities. These folks are paid to worry, and as a result predictability often outweighs potential.

Businesses that show consistency, transferability, and operational clarity inspire more confidence than those that promise a big upside without proof. Therefore, buyer perception plays an incredibly powerful role in shaping deal structure, multiples, and negotiation dynamics. After all, investors control the capital, and confidence determines how freely it is deployed.

From an investor's perspective, emotional detachment and professional process matter. As we've already observed, any business that no longer relies on the founder for day-to-day decision-making, customer relationships, or strategic direction is viewed as more durable and less risky than one that is reliant on the owner's constant presence.

This, then, is where goodwill enters the discussion; not as an accounting byproduct, but as a forward-looking judgment about whether the business can perform without you.

Goodwill is built when systems replace heroics, when teams replace dependency, and when results are repeatable rather than personality-driven. Investors reward businesses that show this transition, whether the buyer is a financial sponsor, a strategic acquirer, or even an internal successor.

Learning to see your business from the investor's perspective will make a significant difference in your ability to help manage both sides of the deal. It will encourage you to prepare as if you were selling to an external investor, even if your ultimate plan is an internal transfer. And it will reduce the likelihood of surprise adjustments during due diligence.

Most importantly, understanding an investor's point of view will help you align your M&A Value Creation™ strategy with how investors define and measure value, rather than by the way owners naturally experience it.

Adopting this perspective will shift your focus. You'll move from asking what you believe is valuable to understanding what buyers will actually pay for. You'll recognize why predictability, transferability, and defensibility matter so much, and why the transferability of goodwill often acts as a hidden multiplier in valuation discussions.

Whether you're selling to an internal buyer, a strategic acquirer, or a financial optimizer, they'll all benefit from this mindset as much as you will.

And here's something else to consider: internal buyers can also benefit from this mindset. Even when a business is not being sold to a strategic acquirer or financial optimizer, aligning the company with what investors want to buy is certain to result in a better, more resilient enterprise. The discipline required to satisfy an investor's expectations will improve outcomes, regardless of who ultimately owns the business.

One thing to keep in mind, though: learning to speak the investor's language does not mean abandoning your identity as an owner. It simply means understanding that investors value clarity over complexity, scalability over effort, and confidence over optimism. When you can translate operational success into investment appeal, you are no longer trying to sell your business. You are, in fact, presenting something investors already want to own.

With this lens in place, the next step becomes exploring additional considerations. That's because investors often weigh factors that may not appear explicitly in financial statements, but do materially influence confidence, risk assessment, and ultimate outcomes.

~ CHAPTER 10 ~

ADDITIONAL INVESTOR CONSIDERATIONS

Let's be obvious for a moment: investors are the people with the money required for a successful outcome. Keeping that reality in mind matters when designing your M&A Value Creation™ strategies, regardless of whether you ultimately sell to an external buyer, an internal successor, or not at all.

Regardless of who the investor is, the one thing that they all truly value is confidence. That's what shows them that the business can continue to perform, decide, and manage risk without depending on any one person or moment in time. They value predictability they can understand, leadership that can be transferred, assets that will continue to perform over the long-term, and operations that run through systems…rather than personalities.

After all, investors may not expect perfection, but they do expect clarity: clear financials, visible risks, and credible paths forward.

Above all, investors are buying into a future they believe is navigable. When a business provides that assurance, investors lean forward. That confidence, more than any single financial metric, is what creates the Invisible Premium™.

Of course, investors can also represent a hurdle. Whether you plan to remain involved after a transaction or depart at closing, an investor is effectively a successor who will eventually sit in the Owner/CEO seat. That transition can be personally challenging for the founder and potentially operationally complex for both parties. Thus negotiations can be difficult, expectations can seemingly shift by the hour, and the presence of outside capital will invariably introduce both new disciplines and constraints.

Therefore, planning matters. Developing and executing a thoughtful M&A Value Creation™ strategy takes time, investment, and perspective. Much of that perspective comes from understanding how others will step into your role and steward what you have built.

Bottom line: a better business produces better outcomes, both for the owner and for its stakeholders.

At the risk of stating the obvious, I should also point out here that investors can also show up in more forms than many owners initially recognize. For example, your investor may be your bank funding future growth rather than acquiring the company. Because while many owners don't think of it that way, when a company takes on debt, it gains a new partner whose interests must be protected and whose rules must be followed.

An investor may also be a minority partner, such as a private equity firm making a partial investment. Or there's an ESOP, where your investors include employees, trustees, and lenders; and are influenced by the IRS rules.

In each case, you are no longer alone in calling the shots.

When you consider it from this angle, it makes sense to design your value creation strategies with investor perceptions in mind. How will they view your business? Have you prepared for due diligence? If you plan to step away, have you thought through both the business transition and your own life after ownership?

From what I've observed over the years, when an owner's hopes and ambitions are aligned with a clear plan for all stakeholders, an exit becomes a purposeful transition, rather than merely being a transaction.

It's also important to recognize that not all buyers are the same. Broadly speaking, there are two types of investors; internal and external. Internal buyers include family members, employees, or partners who may assume ownership. They are taking real financial risks, even when financing structures soften the immediate burden. External buyers include third parties such as private equity firms, family offices, strategic or synergistic acquirers, competitors, independent sponsors, customers, suppliers, or even lenders providing substantial capital.

From a transaction perspective, external investors are often viewed as either financial optimizers or synergistic buyers.

But you need to recognize at the outset that each group evaluates value differently. Understanding these distinctions helps owners think more clearly about positioning, messaging, and optionality. When approached thoughtfully, this awareness can increase your choice of whom to sell to, and improve leverage with each of the possible buyers.

Realistically, designing a value creation strategy that speaks to so many different investor types may feel daunting to the uninitiated. Just remember that the point is not for you to optimize for all of them, but to understand which ones align with your own goals. If you have clarity early on around your ideal investor types, you'll be in a better position to shape your preparation, planning, and expectations long before a transaction is contemplated.

This might also be a good time to again seriously consider having an IntelligentExit® coach as they can help translate your considerations into practical planning. Just recognize that their role is NOT to dictate outcomes, but to help ensure that your objectives, motivations, and constraints are clearly understood and reflected in how the business is positioned.

Naturally, understanding what investors value is only part of the equation. Equally important is recognizing what worries them. This is why the next chapter examines the factors that quietly erode confidence, reduce value, or cause investors to step back altogether.

~ CHAPTER 11 ~

DEAL KILLERS, VALUE REDUCERS AND CONFIDENCE ERODERS

Not all risks are created equal in the eyes of investors. Some stop a transaction outright. Others quietly change pricing, structure, or momentum. Understanding the difference between deal killers, value reducers, and confidence eroders helps explain why transactions collapse, reprice, or drag on long after expectations were set.

Deal Killers (Deal Collapse)

Deal killers make a business un-investable at any price. These are risks that cannot be mitigated through deal structure, insurance, or discounting without threatening ownership, continuity, or enforceability. Investors do not negotiate around deal killers: they walk away.

When investors walk away, it is often late in the deal management process. Sellers do not recover advisory fees, preparation costs, or lost momentum. A deal collapse is expensive for sellers, though professional investors may see walking away as the least costly option. For them, investing in a bad deal is far more expensive than abandoning one.

Common deal killers can include unresolved legal, regulatory, or compliance issues; unclear ownership of assets such as intellectual property, contracts, real estate, or equity; customer, supplier, or revenue concentration that prevents transferability; tax issues or overly aggressive tax positions; ethical or reputational concerns; and situations where due diligence cannot be completed because information is missing or records are unreliable.

IntelligentExit® Note: Deal killers are rarely discovered early in the process. They are revealed under pressure, when options are limited and expectations are already set.

Value Reducers (Deal Repricing)

Value reducers rarely stop a deal, but they will change how investors perceive the company's value. These issues often shift risk back to the seller through price adjustments, contingencies, or deal structures such as earn-outs. Earn-outs defer part of the purchase price and tie payment to future performance, but because earnings cannot be clearly defended, modeled, or replicated, investors understandably look to protect their own interests.

Value reducers frequently include earnings that cannot be traced cleanly to sustainable cash flow; heavy reliance on the owner to drive revenue or operations; aggressively adjusted or poorly documented EBITDA; weak financial controls; or lack of credible forecasting; customer churn; or pricing instability; and underinvestment in systems, working capital, or capital expenditures.

IntelligentExit® Note: What sellers often experience as negotiation tactics are frequently symptoms of insufficient preparation on their part. Repricing is not personal; it reflects uncertainty.

Confidence Eroders (Fixable, but at a Cost)

Confidence erodes quietly. These issues rarely appear in financial statements, but they undermine goodwill and can stall the deal momentum of a deal. While they may seem minor when considered individually, collectively, they will create doubt about whether the business' value will transfer after closing.

Confidence eroders will typically include inconsistent answers or shifting narratives; weak or unproven management teams; poor documentation of processes, intellectual property, or strategic planning; cultural misalignment with the buyer's expectations; disorganized data rooms and reactive communication; and overselling future potential without evidence, such as forecasts that are not documented or tracked.

IntelligentExit® Note: Confidence erosion rarely shows up as rejection. It's more likely to appear as delays, hesitation, and changes in the final offer.

How Different Buyers React

Different buyer types can be expected to respond in dissimilar ways to these risks, based on their motivations and experience.

- Internal buyers often focus first on confidence eroders. Because they already know the business, they may view these issues as a nuisance, rather than as a barrier. What appears to be a deal killer to an external buyer may feel manageable to insiders. That familiarity, however, often comes with a lower price or financing with special terms.
- Financial buyers focus first on value reducers. As their due diligence deepens, deal killers will also reveal themselves. Confidence eroders are usually viewed as fixable, but only at a cost, and that cost is reflected in pricing and deal structure.

- Strategic buyers typically begin by ensuring there are no deal killers. They do not want to acquire problems that could negatively affect their existing operations. As their due diligence progresses, they evaluate confidence eroders and value reducers in the context of their ability to integrate systems, reduce costs, or apply their own infrastructure.

Mind you, all my observations are based on experience, rather than on formal studies. The point of it all, though, is not to categorize buyers rigidly, but rather to help you begin the right conversations early on.

Because preparation changes the outcome of any deals. And even if you disagree with these distinctions, understanding how investors should be expected to react will give you adequate time to address issues before they become expensive.

Then, with a clearer understanding of what will undermine a buyer's confidence and estimation of value for a company, the next chapter looks at the patterns experienced investors will recognize across many transactions. And it discusses what those patterns reveal about businesses that consistently achieve better outcomes.

~ CHAPTER 12 ~

INVESTOR INSIGHTS

It can be useful for entrepreneurs to understand some reasons investors buy businesses - particularly financial optimizers. While this book intentionally avoids becoming too technical or positioning itself merely as a checklist, a basic familiarity with a few Merger & Acquisition (M&A) terms should help you understand how acquirers think and how they frame opportunity, risk, and value.

These concepts are not strategies that you are expected to implement. Rather, they are mechanisms investors use to explain, justify, and manage the future they are buying. Understanding them here will provide you with a glimpse into the investor's mindset.

Financial Optimizer Insights

Financial buyers often describe their objectives using terms such as multiple expansion and earnings accretion. While these sound like technical financial concepts, the underlying work that creates them will be very familiar to you.

- **Multiple expansion**, sometimes described as financial arbitrage, refers to acquiring a business at one valuation multiple and later selling it at a higher one. That increase in multiples rarely comes from financial engineering alone. It is usually the result of reducing risk, improving operational and management predictability, professionalizing systems, and strengthening the business so future performance feels more certain.

Viewed through the lens of the Invisible Premium, multiple expansion is about turning uncertainty into confidence.

- A related concept is **earnings accretion**. This focuses on increasing cash flow and earnings through operational improvements, scale efficiencies, pricing discipline, and sometimes add-on acquisitions. Where multiple expansion reflects how the market values the business, earnings accretion reflects how the business performs. The goal is to make results more durable, repeatable, and defensible.

The work that creates both multiple expansion and earnings accretion is oftentimes the same. Both come from reducing risk, improving predictability, and making performance more transferable. The difference lies in how the buyer measures the results. When that work justifies a higher valuation multiple, it is called multiple expansion. When it produces stronger, more reliable earnings, it is called earnings accretion.

Which helps explain why financial optimizers spend so much time and money on research and due diligence. Because they are not buying history, but rather a future they must be able to explain, defend, implement, and eventually pass on. Their decisions revolve around one thing above all else: confidence.

Strategic Business Objectives

Not all acquisitions are driven strictly by financial optimization. In fact, many buyers pursue transactions to advance broader business objectives.

- In a strategic acquisition, the buyer is often less focused on short-term financial metrics and more concerned with long-term positioning. The acquisition may provide access to new markets, customers, technology, talent, or capabilities that would be slower or more expensive to build internally. These strategies are most often employed by operating companies seeking growth, diversification, or a defensive advantage. Short-term earnings matter, but the long-term outlook matters more. Some private equity portfolio companies also act as strategic acquirers once a platform has been established.
- Defensive acquisitions are designed primarily to reduce risk, rather than accelerate growth. A buyer may seek to protect market share, neutralize a competitor, secure key customers or suppliers, or prevent a rival from acquiring a strategic asset. These deals may not dramatically increase earnings, but they can preserve stability and prevent future disruption. When a buyer perceives a credible market threat, they may even pay a premium for the purchase.

Platform and Add-On Dynamics

- Many entrepreneurs are familiar with roll-up strategies… particularly in private equity. For instance, there's the

platform acquisition, which serves as the foundation for future growth through additional acquisitions. Buyers seek businesses that are well run, scalable, disciplined, and capable of absorbing add-ons. Strong leadership, systems, and market presence are critical. Platform companies often command premium valuations, because they are both transferable and operationally mature.

- **Add-on acquisitions** complement the platform. These businesses are integrated to achieve efficiencies, expand offerings, deepen market penetration, or create cross-selling opportunities. Add-ons may be smaller transactions, but they can be highly attractive when they enhance the performance of the overall enterprise, rather than standing alone. Sometimes, add-ons can also serve strategic purposes.

<u>Other Investor Motivations</u>

- Some buyers pursue **cash-flow-focused acquisitions**. These are businesses that generate predictable and stable cash flow with minimal intervention. They are comfortable to own, and that comfort creates confidence…and value.

- **Turnaround or distressed acquisitions are at the opposite end of the spectrum.** These buyers target underperforming businesses with fixable financial, operational, or structural issues. The perceived upside can be significant, but so is the risk. Uncertainty is priced aggressively into the deal, and once the transaction closes, control typically shifts decisively to the acquirer.

Finally, some acquirers pursue **long-term hold acquisitions**. This approach is common among family offices, though not exclusive to them. The focus is on long-term performance, cultural alignment, and continuity, rather than near-term optimization. These buyers value businesses that have weathered market cycles, demonstrate durable values, and can compound value over time. Sellers who care deeply about legacy and stakeholder outcomes are often drawn to these buyers.

These are not the only acquisition motivations, of course, but they represent some of the most common patterns in the middle market. Understanding them does not require you to adopt an investor's playbook. It simply helps you appreciate how different buyers define opportunity, and why they value certain attributes more than others.

Taken together, these insights reveal a common thread across investor types: confidence in what comes next. The final chapter of this section summarizes how the investor's point of view shapes valuation, deal structure, and outcomes, and why understanding that perspective is essential to an IntelligentExit®.

~ CHAPTER 13 ~

FROM THE INVESTOR'S POINT OF VIEW

In this section, you've learned that the investor's point of view is more than a perspective. It is, in fact, a lens through which decisions are evaluated, risks are weighed, and value is ultimately assigned.

This section's purpose was not intended to be academic or technical, but rather to start a conversation. The conversation is one you can have with your IntelligentExit® coach, your M&A transaction advisor, and other trusted counselors/advisors as you prepare for your professional and personal next steps.

I provided this section recognizing that understanding how investors think will allow you to test your decisions before the market does.

By stepping into the investor's point of view, you've seen how businesses are evaluated long before an offer is made. You've learned why it matters to align your M&A Value Creation™ strategies with an investor's priorities. You now understand how perceived risk can quietly lower valuation, change deal structure, or delay outcomes. And you've also seen how anticipating investor questions and concerns will strengthen your position at the negotiating table.

Arguably, one of the most important insights you've gained from this section has been the role of goodwill. Because no matter what anyone tells you, goodwill is neither a line item nor an afterthought. It is, in fact, the judgment that investors make about whether a business will continue to perform after ownership in a business changes.

After all, when goodwill is transferable, it enhances a company's value. When it is strictly personal or fragile, it becomes a source of huge risk.

The investor point of view transforms your IntelligentExit® from an internal planning exercise into an external advantage. When you learn to see what investors see and address what they will probably flag as problematic, you are no longer simply preparing to sell. Rather, you are preparing to compete for the best outcome in selling your business, while dramatically improving the odds of getting better results.

Keep in mind, though, that thinking like an investor does not mean abandoning your own identity as an owner. It means recognizing that perception drives pricing, confidence drives structure, and predictability drives value. When those elements align, your business is certain to command stronger offers and cleaner deals.

Key Takeaways

- The investor point of view defines how value is perceived and priced.
- Investors prioritize predictable, transferable returns over unproven potential.
- Aligning strategy with investor priorities improves readiness and outcomes.

- Anticipating investor concerns strengthens confidence and negotiating on positions.
- Goodwill is a critical driver of value, and often explains why one business commands a premium over another.
- The IntelligentExit® platform helps build a business investors want to buy, rather than one you have to sell.

Now that you have a clearer understanding of how investors interpret value and risk, the next section will help you explore how goodwill is intentionally designed and reinforced. These chapters focus on designing goodwill, shaping confidence before it is tested, and ensuring that what you've built endures beyond the transaction itself.

PART III
DESIGNING GOODWILL

What You Will Learn
About Designing Goodwill
for Your Company

Most owners encounter goodwill at the end of a transaction, often as a residual number on a balance sheet or a line item explained by an advisor. In reality, goodwill is neither accidental nor abstract. It is the economic expression of a buyer's confidence that the value of a business will continue after ownership of the firm changes hands.

In this section you will learn how goodwill is formed long before a deal begins, and why it plays a central role in why some businesses command better offers than others.

Designing goodwill begins with an understanding of how buyers assess risk. Buyers do not simply evaluate performance; they also carefully examine durability, transferability, and trust. They ask whether earnings are real and repeatable; whether leadership and relationships will hold; and whether the business can function without the current owner at its center. When those questions are answered clearly, goodwill expands. When they are not, goodwill is discounted or protected against.

Within the IntelligentExit® platform, goodwill is treated as a strategic outcome, rather than as a negotiation framework. It is built deliberately through value creation, risk reduction, and thoughtful preparation. By addressing the factors that undermine confidence before a transaction begins, owners influence how buyers experience the business and determine how much they will pay for what cannot be fully captured on financial statements.

This section reframes goodwill as something that can be intentionally designed. It explores how buyers form conviction; why certain risks quietly erode value; and how owners can shape goodwill well before valuation discussions begin.

~ CHAPTER 14 ~

DESIGNING GOODWILL

Most business owners first encounter the word *goodwill* when they are already sitting across the table from a buyer. An accountant explains that goodwill is more than a non-profit that you donate your old clothing to, and in fact represents the premium paid - above tangible assets - when you're selling the business. The lawyers nod, and the number is typed into the purchase agreement…even though the buyer's judgment behind that number was formed LONG before the meeting began.

In fact, by the time goodwill appears as a line item, it is no longer being created; it is merely being recorded.

But what often goes unspoken is that goodwill is not an accounting construct at all. Rather, it is the economic expression of a buyer's confidence that the value of a business will continue long after ownership in the business has changed hands.

The fact is a long time before goodwill appears on any balance sheet, it exists in the buyer's mind as a forward-looking assessment of risk, continuity, and trust.

Goodwill Begins with Buyer Risk

Here's the thing: buyers do not simply evaluate historical performance, but actually whether that performance is durable over the long-term. They ask whether earnings are real and repeatable; whether advantages can be defended; and whether the business can function without the owner at the center of every decision.

From where the buyer is sitting, risk is practical rather than abstract, and there is absolutely no emotion involved on their part. It shows up when they're asking questions like:

- Will the company's customers stay when ownership changes?
- Will the margins hold without the founder's involvement?
- Will key relationships transfer readily to the new owner?
- Will systems, processes, and decision rights function properly, regardless of who is in charge independently?
- Will the management team operate with consistent discipline and judgment when there's a new owner?

When these questions are answered clearly, confidence grows. When they are not, buyers compensate for incomplete information by making lower offers; providing tighter terms; insisting on earn-outs and/or holdbacks; or by walking away from the deal altogether.

Thus the value of your goodwill will expand or contract based on how convincingly and thoroughly you're able to answer these questions.

Performance is Necessary, but Not Sufficient

Strong financial performance is essential, of course, but it is rarely decisive on its own. Buyers expect financial results to explain what has already happened, while goodwill reflects their judgment about what is likely to happen next.

Let's go back to the Tale of Two Companies, where we started this discussion.

Two companies look the same on paper, but one sells for $10 million and the other for $7 million. What do you think the buyer saw that the financials did not show?

The reality is that these two businesses reported similar earnings, yet commanded very different offers. The difference in a case like this would typically lie in how buyers interpret what sits behind those earnings. Businesses that rely heavily on personal relationships, undocumented know-how, or founder-centric decision-making may perform well today, yet feel fragile tomorrow. Others, with comparable results, may feel stable, transferable, and resilient.

Goodwill is the premium that buyers will willingly pay when they believe the company's financial performance is not only strong, but sustainable over the long-term.

Designing Confidence, Not Negotiating It

Within the IntelligentExit® platform, goodwill is not an accounting byproduct or something won at the negotiating table. Rather, it is an expression of confidence that is designed over time; not something argued for at the end of a deal.

Designing goodwill means intentionally shaping how a buyer experiences the business long before valuation discussions begin. It involves reducing uncertainty, strengthening transferability, and showing that the business can thrive independently of any one individual.

Deriving maximum value from goodwill does not require perfect operations or flawless execution, either. All it requires is clarity.

Because buyers do NOT need certainty. They need confidence that their risks are understood, being managed, and unlikely to surprise them after closing.

Trust me when I say that surprises are fine for birthday parties, but should be kept out of business settings whenever possible.

How Goodwill Quietly Compounds

The individual elements influencing goodwill often feel familiar to owners. Trade secrets, brand strength, recurring revenue, leadership discipline, management depth, and customer concentration are all commonly discussed topics.

What is easy to miss in this conversation, though, is how these elements interact in a buyer's mind. When they reinforce one another, confidence compounds. Doubt obviously emerges, though, when they conflict.

And it's important to recognize that a strong brand paired with weak management depth raises questions about the overall business. Recurring revenue without customer stickiness is sure to invite skepticism. Even having impressive margins without documented processes can feel fragile.

But goodwill will reflect how these signs can or cannot align into a coherent picture of future performance.

Why Some Businesses Get Better Offers

Clearly, businesses that get better offers do so because buyers experience them as lower risk, and not just because the owners negotiated harder. The premium is earned through preparation, consistency, and alignment between what the business promises and what it can reliably - and repeatedly - deliver.

Goodwill, then, is the buyer's way of pricing that confidence.

This chapter shifts the focus from how goodwill is recorded to how buyers actually think about it. You should be taking away opportunities for intentionally shaping goodwill, and understanding why goodwill is discounted when a buyer's confidence erodes.

You've seen how owners who address risks early on can often experience not only higher offers, but cleaner deal terms and a much greater certainty of closing.

Which is why - in the chapters that follow - we're going to explore the specific elements that contribute to this confidence and how they interact to form the invisible premium buyers are willing to pay.

~ CHAPTER 15 ~

FACTORS THAT AFFECT GOODWILL

When an entrepreneur is considering exiting their business, goodwill is one of the most misunderstood (and most valuable) components of the transaction. As I noted earlier, you will not find goodwill listed on your financial statements. Instead, it reflects the buyer's judgment about the economic value of the business, and whether that value will continue after ownership of the business changes hands.

As we've already discussed, goodwill is not created at closing in an IntelligentExit®. It is actually built long before a business goes to market, and its value is earned through credibility, transferability, and trust.

Buyers assign goodwill when they believe earnings are real and traceable to cash flow. Financial performance alone is not enough, as earnings must be understandable, defensible, and capable of continuing without questions or guesswork. When earnings are overly adjusted, poorly documented, or difficult to reconcile, buyers reduce goodwill first, even when reported profitability appears strong.

The following are key factors that influence goodwill, and should be addressed well before a business is offered for sale.

Earnings Credibility

Goodwill begins with confidence in earnings. Buyers assess whether reported performance reflects economic reality, asking whether;

- Earnings can be traced clearly to cash flow
- Margins are consistent
- Revenues are predictable

They also evaluate whether adjustments are defensible and whether normalization has been completed conservatively.

Ultimately, buyers want to know whether future earnings can reasonably be expected to continue based on historical and current performance. Thus, goodwill reflects future economic benefits…but when buyers doubt the quality of those earnings, goodwill shrinks.

Even if profits are strong.

IntelligentExit® perspective:

Earnings quality is treated as a trust issue, rather than merely a financial one.

- **Transferability of Leadership and Know-how**

Buyers closely evaluate whether leadership and institutional knowledge will remain intact after the transaction is completed. They consider the depth and credibility of the management team; whether strategic planning has been documented; and whether results have been tracked. They assess how dependent the business is on the founder for sales, customer relationships, and key decisions.

Thus goodwill collapses when buyers fear that the company's critical knowledge or leadership will be walking out the door after the closing.

IntelligentExit® perspective:
Management transferability is a foundational readiness and value-creation factor.

- **Brand Equity and Reputation**
  Brand equity plays a central role in goodwill, because it represents trust that has already been earned. Buyers look for documented customer loyalty, a market reputation that extends beyond the founder's personal brand, and a consistent brand promise that is both understood and delivered. They also evaluate whether reputational or ethical risks exist beneath the surface.

  As you've undoubtedly already observed, brand equity is a monetized version of brand trust. High customer retention reduces perceived risk and increases goodwill.

  IntelligentExit® perspective:
  Brand trust is treated as part of the company's infrastructure, rather than just being marketing fluff.

- **Customer and Revenue Stability**
  Goodwill grows when future revenue feels repeatable and

resilient, rather than opportunistic. Buyers assess customer concentration, the durability of long-term relationships, and whether contracts are transferable. They look for minimized customer and supplier churn, recurring renewals, and pricing stability. A diversified customer base across industries further strengthens confidence.

IntelligentExit® Perspective:
You don't fix revenue quality in due diligence; you prove it there.

- **Governance, Controls, and Operating Discipline**
  Governance is one of the least visible, but most powerful, drivers of goodwill. Buyers pay attention to how quickly financials are closed and reported. Whether those internal controls are documented and followed, and whether governance structures such as boards or advisory groups exist in name only, rather than in actual practice. They evaluate decision-making discipline and the consistency of management execution, recognizing that sloppy governance raises integration risks and erodes goodwill.

IntelligentExit® Perspective:
Governance is a confidence builder; not bureaucratic oversight.

- **Intellectual Property and Defensibility**
  Goodwill increases when buyers believe competitive advantages will persist after the sale. This includes:
  - Clear ownership and protection of intellectual property
  - Documented proprietary processes
  - Established barriers to entry, and

- Deliberate development of brand trust both internally and externally

IntelligentExit® perspective:
Intellectual property is elevated as a strategic value driver, rather than merely as a legal concern.

- **Cultural Alignment and Values**
  Cultural alignment affects deal continuity more than most owners expect. This is because buyers evaluate whether leadership styles, decision-making norms, and values align with how THEY operate.

  Thus this is not about slogans or personalities. It's about how people are treated, accountability functions, and whether employees are likely to remain after the business has been sold.

  Also bear in mind that cultural friction increases the risks of a newly-acquired business integrating smoothly into the buyer's structure of risk. Buyers who sense a misalignment will quietly discount value when negotiating their offer.

  IntelligentExit® Perspective:
  Culture is addressed as deal continuity. It's counter-productive to see it as part of the post-close cleanup process.

- **Narrative Consistency and Trust**
  Goodwill is reinforced when the story of the business is consistent and credible.

> Because buyers expect alignment across management, advisors, and the data room, transparency matters…especially when challenges are known to exist.
>
> Disclosing negative factors early - and before a buyer discovers them - helps build trust, preserves narrative control, and engenders goodwill.

Confidence will naturally follow.

IntelligentExit® Perspective:
Narrative integrity is treated as risk management.

Here's the bottom line: goodwill is one of the most important contributors to a successful outcome when selling your business. It is shaped by how convincingly a business shows that value will endure beyond the founder being in the room.

Author's Note:

In a prior transaction, we identified a significant dip in sales during a historical period. By disclosing the issue early and transparently (and before the buyer uncovered it themselves), we controlled the narrative and preserved trust throughout the process.

~ CHAPTER 16 ~

DESIGNING GOODWILL

Let me be blunt: this section establishes that goodwill is neither an accounting outcome nor a negotiating tactic, but rather a designed result. Buyers assign a value to goodwill when they believe that a certain amount of value will endure after ownership of the business changes hands.

That belief is shaped by how their risk is reduced, how transferable the business becomes, and how consistently confident they are that the numbers will stand up under scrutiny.

Thus by using the IntelligentExit® platform and workflow, goodwill shifts from something sellers hope for at the end of a deal to something they deliberately build.

Key Takeaways

- Goodwill reflects a buyer's belief that value will survive and transfer after the owner exits
- Deal killers eliminate goodwill, value reducers compress it, and confidence eroders quietly weaken it

- Strong financial performance alone does not create goodwill; credibility and durability do
- Leadership transferability is as important to goodwill as earnings quality
- Brand reputation, governance discipline, and intellectual property compound buyer confidence
- Goodwill grows when risk is reduced early, not negotiated late

PART IV
WHAT YOU'VE LEARNED ABOUT THE INVISIBLE PREMIUM

Across these sections, one idea has remained consistent: better offers are not the result of a single decision or moment. They are, in fact, the outcome of how a buyer experiences the overall business being sold.

From an investor's point of view, value is not limited to what can be measured on a financial statement. Buyers interpret signs about durability, transferability, and trust to form a judgment about whether future earnings will persist after ownership of the business changes hands. That judgment quietly shapes price, deal structure, and certainty of close long before negotiations begin.

Goodwill, viewed through this lens, is not an accounting byproduct or a negotiating prize, but rather an expression of confidence. When familiar elements align - strong operations, defensible advantages, recurring revenues, capable leadership, and reduced reliance on the owner - confidence compounds. When they do not, buyers protect themselves through discounts, conditions, hesitation, or walking away from the deal altogether.

The invisible premium emerges when a business consistently shows that its value will endure. This helps explain why businesses with similar financial performance can command very different offers. Because buyers recognize they are not only buying earnings, but are also acquiring continuity and confidence in what comes next.

This collection is intentionally nonprescriptive. Its purpose is not to tell owners what to do, but to provide insights into the mind of the buyer and help clarify how buyers decide what they're willing to pay for a given company. By understanding how value is interpreted from the outside, owners seeking to sell can gain a clearer view of where their risk may be overstated. They can find where confidence can be strengthened, and where intentional decisions - made well before a transaction - can materially influence the outcome of their negotiations.

And the bottom line? Businesses that ultimately get better offers do so because they make themselves worthy of greater investment. That feeling is not accidental, but is shaped over time through alignment, preparation, and a clear understanding of what buyers truly value when their own future is on the line.

A Note to Professional Advisors

This collection is written for owner/CEOs, but it is intended to support collaborative work with their advisors. The purpose of this material is not to prescribe solutions, but to provide shared language for discussing how buyers interpret intangible assets such as trade secrets, brand trust, and recurring revenue.

When owners understand why buyers pay premiums, they are better positioned to engage advisors earlier, follow advice more consistently, and invest in the right initiatives at the right time.

The IntelligentExit® Coach is not expected to replace professional expertise. Instead, the role is to support clearer framing, better alignment, and more effective execution of advisor-led solutions.

Because decades of hard-won business experience in the front-line trenches has taught me that effective exits are rarely the result of a single discipline: they are the result of alignment.™

Acknowledgements

This book reflects more than five decades of firsthand experience as an executive and owner/CEO of family-owned businesses, as well as my work alongside owner/CEOs as an M&A transaction advisor. It also draws on years of collaboration with professional advisors and direct negotiation with investors navigating the complexities of building, transitioning, and exiting privately held businesses.

Along the way I have benefited from the insights of many professionals, clients, and peers whose perspectives helped shape the thinking reflected in these pages. In preparing this manuscript, I made use of modern research and editorial tools to support accuracy, idea development, and clarity of expression. These tools assisted in refining language and testing concepts, but all frameworks, interpretations, and conclusions presented here are my own.

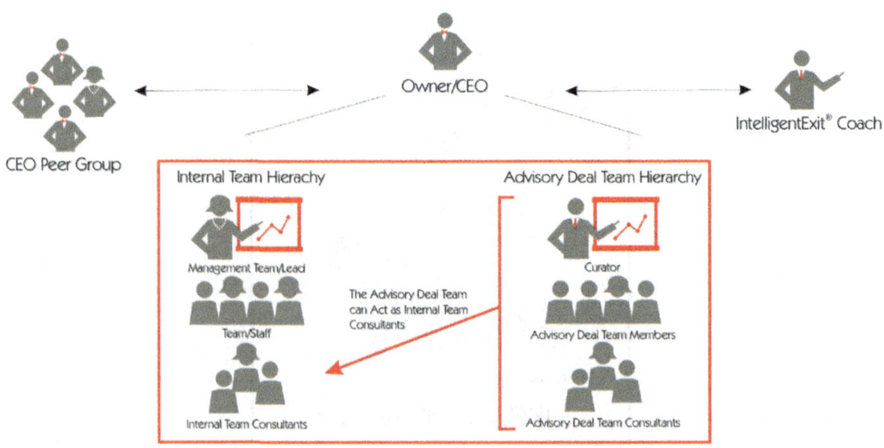

ABOUT THE AUTHOR

Meet John C. Henberger, Jr.
M&A Value Creation™ Coach

As a former CEO, M&A transaction advisor, and non-stop entrepreneur, John C. Henberger Jr. brings more than five decades of experience helping fellow entrepreneurs understand how goodwill is created beyond the financial statement.

He developed the IntelligentExit® Platform to help owners reduce risk, build trust, and strengthen the intangible drivers that influence buyer confidence, pricing, and transaction outcomes.

Watch for his new book *Build a Better Business...And Sell It for More!*™ - THE BUILDING VALUE EDITION.

You can reach John for interviews, consulting, or bulk purchases of this book at john@henberger.com or www.henberger.com. You'll also find him at either www.intelligentexit.com, or online at linkedin.com/in/johnhenberger.

Made in the USA
Monee, IL
12 September 2026

62974218R00059